Sharon Boisvert

50 WAYS WITH
POTATOES

50 WAYS WITH

POTATOES

ROSEMARY WADEY

LANSDOWNE

Published by Lansdowne Publishing Pty Ltd
Level 5, 70 George Street, Sydney NSW 2000, Australia

© Copyright: Lansdowne Publishing Pty Ltd 1995
© Copyright design: Lansdowne Publishing Pty Ltd 1995

First published by Weldon Publishing 1991
Reprinted 1994, 1995(twice)

Managing Director: Jane Curry
Production Manager: Sally Stokes
Publishing Manager: Deborah Nixon
Project Coordinator/Editor: Bronwyn Hilton
Designed by Kathie Baxter Smith
Photography by Andrew Elton
Food Styling by Mary Harris
Recipes typeset in Granjon by Character, North Sydney
Printed in Singapore by Tien Wah Press (Pte) Ltd

British Library Cataloguing-in-Publication Data
A catalogue record for this book is available from the British Library

ISBN 1-86302-414 X

All rights reserved. Subject to the Copyright Act 1968,
no part of this publication may be reproduced, stored in a retrieval
system, or transmitted in any form, or by any means, electronic,
mechanical, photocopying, recording or otherwise, without the prior
written permission of the publisher.

Front cover photograph: Stilton and Chives Filled Baked Jacket Potato, recipe page 102
Page 2: Potato and Artichoke Salad, recipe page 58
Page 8 & 9: Herbed Potato Parcel, recipe page 38
Back cover photograph: Picadillo, recipe page 54

CONTENTS

Introduction 6

The Recipes 9

INTRODUCTION

Potatoes originate from the same botanical family as Deadly Nightshade, and are a native of the Andes region in South America. A staple in the diet of the Incas of Peru, the Spanish first brought them to Europe in the sixteenth century. Being something of a curiosity at first, potatoes were held in suspicion and eaten only by the rich. By the eighteenth century, potatoes were popular at the courts of Frederick the Great of Prussia and Louis XVI of France and, by the nineteenth century, they were common on the tables of the poorer classes. Indeed, the critical importance of the potato in the Irish diet could not be denied when in the mid 1840's, a failure in the potato harvest led to widespread famine and disaster. Today the potato, a common garden and commercial vegetable, is cultivated in hundreds of varieties and eaten all over the world.

An ideal ingredient for healthy, modern eating, potatoes are loved as hearty fare by meat-eaters, vegetarians and vegans alike. Nutritionalists have shown that potatoes are not the fattening food they were once thought to be. In fact, boiled new potatoes in their skins, yield only 22 calories (less than 100 kilojoules) per 1 oz (30 g). With this good news for the weight conscious comes even better news for the health conscious. Potatoes are an inexpensive source of carbohydrates and nutrients — including vitamins C and A, protein, iron, thiamine, niacin, calcium and of course dietary fibre and, in dishes where potato skins are left on, the nutritional value is increased further.

It is the cell structure of the potato that determines its texture when cooked. Waxy potatoes have a lower starch content and will boil and deep–fry beautifully, but are unsuitable for baking or mashing. Floury varieties are ideal for purees and mashing because they collapse during boiling. Numerous kinds of potatoes with varying characteristics can be grown, and these, as well as the times they are available, differ greatly from country to country depending on climatic conditions and terrain. Varieties are often more simply classified according to two main types: the Early potatoes or 'Earlies' and the Maincrop varieties.

Earlies or 'new' potatoes herald the beginning of summer, except in particularly warm climates where they are available all year. When first lifted,

Earlies are ideal for boiling — and they are best boiled with the skins left on — being firm and waxy with a real 'earthy' taste. As they mature they become softer, the waxy texture disappears and the skin thickens. To check for true Earlies, rub the skin with your finger and it should flake off. This type of potato should not be bought in bulk, as they do not store well.

Maincrop potatoes should be bought and stored for use over a period time. The skins vary in hue, from pale cream to a deep chestnut, and from a pale pink to a deep pinkish purple. The flesh varies too, from off white to deep cream to yellow. In some countries you can buy 'Second Earlies', which are a true mix between both types. Some of those varieties are classed as adequate all-rounders.

Sweet potato is a variety of potato that has a slightly sweet taste. They are native to Central America but now grow world wide in suitable sub–tropical climates. They are much larger than normal potatoes, often elongated, with a thicker skin of red or white and a coarser textured flesh, varying from off white to deep yellow. They can be baked in their skins, but otherwise are best peeled, and can be used in place of, or mixed with ordinary potatoes. As you will see, they are well represented in many recipes throughout this book — try Picadillo, recipe page 54, a tasty treat from the Caribbean or Sweet Potato Bake, recipe page 94.

The best quality potatoes should look clean, well-shaped and firm, free from cuts and blemishes and definitely should have no green parts or shoots apparent. Light can turn potatoes green, and both warmth and dampness may cause sprouting and shrivelling as well as hastening the rotting process. Accordingly, they should be stored carefully in a dark, cool, but frost–free place with plenty of air circulation. Never store potatoes in plastic bags and keep them well away from strong smells as they tend to absorb odours. It is best to buy little and often if you don't have a suitable storage place.

Potatoes are a most versatile vegetable and this collection of recipes gives you a chance to enjoy the virtually limitless, exciting ways they can be prepared. Handy hints have been included, see page 110, to ensure your potatoes are prepared to perfection. Choose from the tempting selection of potato snacks, starters, main courses and accompaniments that have been influenced by various international cuisines, and be sure to please your family and guests.

THE RECIPES

BOXTY

2 lb (900 g) potatoes, peeled
salt and freshly ground black
    pepper
3 cups (12 oz, 350 g) all-purpose
    (plain) flour
1/2 oz (15 g) baking powder
1 level teaspoon celery salt
4 oz (100 g) softened butter or
    margarine
sesame seeds, poppy seeds or
    pumpkin seeds to decorate

Cook half the potatoes in boiling salted water for about 15–20 minutes until tender. Drain thoroughly. Alternatively, cut into cubes and put into a microwave-proof dish with 3 tablespoons water, cover and cook on maximum (100%) for 9 minutes, stirring halfway through cooking. Mash potatoes until very smooth adding salt and pepper to taste.

Preheat oven to moderate (350°F, 180°C, Gas Mark 4). Coarsely grate remaining potatoes. Remove as much moisture as possible with a clean cloth or paper towel, combine with mashed potatoes, flour, baking powder, celery salt and butter. Mix well.

Turn dough onto a lightly floured surface and divide into four. Shape each into a round about 1/4 inch (5 mm) thick and mark into quarters with a sharp knife. Place on well-greased baking sheets, sprinkle with sesame seeds and cook in oven for about 40 minutes until risen and golden brown.

Serve hot or warm, broken into quarters with butter, cheese, pickles and salads.

Preparation time about 20 minutes

Cooking time about 40 minutes

Makes 4 (or 16 quarters)

Note: Try using a mixture of ordinary potatoes and sweet potatoes for this bread; mash one type, grate the other and combine as above.

BRANDADE

10–12 oz (300–350 g) skinless,
  boneless white fish (cod,
  haddock, sole or similar fish)
1/3 cup (5 fl oz, 150 ml) milk
salt and freshly ground black
  pepper
1 small onion, peeled and finely
  chopped
6 oz (175 g) boiled potatoes, peeled
  and diced
2 cloves garlic, crushed
2 tablespoons olive oil
2 tablespoons lemon juice
2–4 tablespoons heavy (double)
  cream, sour cream or crème
  fraîche
capers to garnish
tomato slices to garnish

Poach fish in milk and seasonings for about 5 minutes until tender. Cool in the cooking juices and remove. Flake fish, discarding any bones and skin.

Put onion and potatoes into a blender or food processor and process until smooth. Add garlic and fish and continue mixing until quite smooth.

Add olive oil, half the lemon juice and 2 tablespoons of cream and mix to a smooth texture. Add extra lemon juice and cream, if necessary, to obtain a thick spreading consistency and season to taste.

Turn into a serving dish and chill thoroughly. Garnish with capers and sliced tomatoes and serve with hot toast, crackers or crusty bread.

Preparation time about 25 minutes

Cooking time 5 minutes

Serves 4

Note: Brandade will keep in the refrigerator for up to 48 hours. It also makes great sandwich filling, together with salad ingredients.

BUBBLE AND SQUEAK

12 oz (350 g) any cooked
  vegetables — carrot, parsnip,
  zucchini (courgette), sprouts,
  beans, peas, marrow,
  mushrooms, bell pepper
  (capsicum), cauliflower or
  broccoli
2 tablespoons oil or butter
1 large onion, peeled and thinly
  sliced
1 clove garlic, crushed
1 1/2 lb (675 g) potatoes, mashed
12 oz (350 g) cooked shredded
  cabbage (green or white)
4 oz (100 g) streaky bacon slices,
  crisply fried and crumbled
  (optional)

Use any boiled or roast leftover potatoes you may have, simply slice or dice them. Cut the other vegetables into manageable pieces.

Heat oil in a large frying pan and fry onion and garlic gently until soft but barely browned. Add mashed potato and stir-fry for about 5 minutes. Add cabbage and cook for a few minutes more, stirring well to prevent sticking as the mixture begins to brown. Add other vegetables and continue until well browned.

Pat the mixture down into a fairly flat cake and cook until golden brown underneath. Finish off under a moderate broiler (grill) for a few minutes so the top is browned.

For individual Bubble and Squeak patties, combine all ingredients as described above and divide into four portions. Shape each into a cake and fry on both sides until golden brown.

Serve cut into wedges and sprinkled with crumbled bacon.

Preparation time about 10 minutes

Cooking time about 20 minutes

Serves 4

Note: Traditionally this dish uses any cooked leftover vegetables. The essentials are onion, potato and a green vegetable but do experiment with a greater variety of ingredients.

CHEESE AND POTATO SCONES

10 oz (300 g) potatoes, peeled and
    roughly cut
salt and freshly ground black
    pepper
1 1/2 cups (6 oz, 175 g) self rising
    flour
1/4 level teaspoon baking soda
    (bicarbonate of soda)
4 level tablespoons grated
    parmesan or pecorino cheese
1 level tablespoon freshly chopped
    tarragon or 1 level teaspoon
    dried tarragon
2 eggs, lightly beaten
little milk to glaze

Variation: Use different herbs; replace parmesan cheese with finely grated blue cheese; add 2 tablespoons chopped sun-dried tomatoes or stuffed olives, or add 2 oz (50 g) crisp, crumbled bacon.

Cook potatoes in boiling salted water for about 15–20 minutes until tender and drain thoroughly; or place in a microwave dish with 3 tablespoons water and a little salt, cover and cook on maximum (100%) for 9 minutes, stirring halfway through cooking. Mash until smooth, without adding extra milk or butter. Cool a little but not until cold.

Sift flour and baking soda together and work into potatoes with 3 tablespoons of cheese, tarragon and eggs. This can be done by hand, in a blender or food processor or by using a hand-held electric mixer.

Preheat oven to moderate (375°F, 190°C, Gas Mark 5).

Turn dough onto a lightly floured surface, knead lightly until smooth then pat out the dough to an even layer of about 3/4 inch (2 cm) thickness. Cut into circles or squares of about 1 1/2 inch (4 cm) using a floured cutter.

Transfer carefully to a greased and floured baking sheet. Brush tops with milk and sprinkle with remaining cheese. Cook in oven for 10–15 minutes or until well risen and golden brown. Cool on a wire rack.

Preparation time 20 minutes

Cooking time 10–15 minutes

Makes 8–10

Note: These scones may be frozen for up to 4 weeks. Once thawed, reheat gently before serving.

CRAB AND POTATO SALAD

1 lb (450 g) potatoes in their skins,
scrubbed

salt and freshly ground black
pepper

2 tablespoons French dressing
(see page 58)

2 tablespoons sour cream, fromage
frais or plain (natural) yogurt

1/4–1/2 level teaspoon medium
curry powder or ground cumin

4 oz (100 g) snow peas (mange
tout) or sugar snap peas,
trimmed

6 oz (175 g) zucchini (courgettes),
trimmed and cut into narrow
sticks

4–6 oz (100–175 g) baby corn

1 dressed crab, or 6 oz (175 g)
canned or frozen crabmeat,
thawed

mixed lettuce leaves

4 crab claws to garnish

Cook potatoes in boiling salted water for about 10–15 minutes until tender. Alternatively, place potatoes in a microwave-proof bowl with 3 tablespoons water and a sprinkling of salt and microwave on maximum (100%) for 10 minutes. Drain, and let cool a little. Cut into thick slices and place in a bowl.

Whisk together the French dressing, sour cream, seasonings and curry powder until emulsified. Add to sliced potato, toss well and leave until cold.

Meanwhile, cook snow peas and zucchini in boiling water for about 2 minutes until tender. Drain and rinse under cold running water. Cook baby corn in boiling water for about 5 minutes until tender and drain.

Flake crab meat and combine with snow peas, zucchini and baby corn and season lightly.

Arrange a selection of lettuce leaves on four individual plates and spoon the potato salad across one side of the plate and the crab mixture across the other. Garnish each salad with a crab claw.

Preparation time about 25 minutes

Cooking time 10–15 minutes

Serves 4

CREAMED POTATO AND PUMPKIN SOUP

2 oz (50 g) butter or margarine
2 onions, peeled and sliced
1 clove garlic, crushed
2 lb (900 g) pumpkin or butternut
    squash, peeled, seeded and
    diced
12 oz (350 g) potatoes, peeled and
    diced
1$1/2$ level teaspoons tomato puree
2$1/2$ cups (20 fl oz, 600 ml) chicken
    or vegetable stock
salt and freshly ground black
    pepper
2 teaspoons lemon or lime juice
$1/2$ level teaspoon ground allspice
2 $1/2$ cups (20 fl oz, 600 ml) milk
6 tablespoons sour cream
freshly chopped cilantro (fresh
    coriander leaves) or parsley to
    garnish

Melt butter in a large saucepan and sauté onions and garlic very gently until soft but not browned.

Add pumpkin and potatoes and cook for a few minutes, then add tomato puree, stock, seasonings, lemon juice and allspice and bring to a boil. Cover pan and simmer gently for about 40 minutes or until very tender.

Sieve soup, or puree in a blender or food processor and return to a clean pan.

Add milk and bring back to a boil, whisking continuously. Simmer for 2–3 minutes. Adjust seasonings and stir in sour cream.

Reheat and serve sprinkled generously with cilantro.

Preparation time about 15 minutes

Cooking time 45–50 minutes

Serves 6

Note: Without the addition of cream this soup may be frozen for up to 3 months.

CREAMY BEET AND POTATO BORSCH

2 oz (50 g) butter or margarine
2 large onions, peeled and chopped
1 large carrot, peeled and chopped
1 lb (450 g) cooked beets
    (beetroot), diced
12 oz (350 g) potatoes, peeled and
    diced
grated rind of 1/2 lemon
2 tablespoons lemon juice
5 cups (40 fl oz, 1.1 l) beef or
    vegetable stock
salt and freshly ground black
    pepper
1/2 level teaspoon ground
    fenugreek
1 1/4 cups (10 fl oz, 300 ml) milk
1–2 level tablespoons finely
    chopped chives or scallion
    (shallot) tops
2/3 cup (5 fl oz, 150 ml) sour cream,
    plain (natural) yogurt or crème
    fraîche

Melt butter in a pan and sauté onion and carrot very gently, stirring frequently for about 7–8 minutes until beginning to soften but not brown.

Add beets, potato, lemon rind and juice, stock, seasonings and fenugreek and bring to a boil. Cover and simmer for about 30 minutes until very tender. Cool slightly.

Sieve the soup or puree in a blender or food processor. Return to a clean pan.

Add milk and bring back to a boil. Adjust seasonings and stir in chives.

Serve each bowl of soup with a spoonful of sour cream or crème fraîche swirled through.

Preparation time about 15 minutes

Cooking time about 35 minutes

Serves 6

Note: This soup may be frozen without the addition of milk or cream for up to 3 months.

CROQUETTES

2 lb (900 g) potatoes or sweet
    potatoes, peeled and cubed
salt and freshly ground black
    pepper
1 egg, beaten
1/3 cup (3 oz, 75 g) dried golden or
    wholemeal breadcrumbs or
    pumpkin seeds or chopped nuts
    (hazelnuts, almonds or mixed)
Fillings:
8 small carrots, peeled and cooked
    or 4 oz (100 g) camembert or
    Stilton cheese or 4 oz (100 g)
    cooked leaf spinach, chopped
oil for deep-frying
fresh parsley to garnish

Cook potato in boiling salted water for 10–15 minutes until tender; or place in a microwave-proof dish with 3 tablespoons of water and a sprinkling of salt, cover and cook in a microwave oven on maximum (100%) for 10 minutes. Drain potatoes and mash until smooth, season well and beat in egg. Leave to cool.

For plain croquettes: Divide the mixture into 8–12 portions and form each into a barrel shape, using wet hands to prevent sticking. Roll in breadcrumbs, nuts or pumpkin seeds to coat evenly and chill until ready to cook.

Heat oil in a pan suitable for deep-frying to 350°F (180°C) or heat about 1 inch (2.5 cm) of oil in a frying pan. Add croquettes a few at a time and cook until golden brown, about 4 minutes. Turn several times if shallow-frying to brown evenly. Drain on paper towels and keep warm while cooking the remainder.

For filled croquettes: Divide the mixture into 8 portions and shape each around a cooked carrot, piece of cheese or portion of spinach to completely enclose the filling. Coat and cook as for plain croquettes.

Garnish with fresh parsley and serve hot as an accompaniment or snack.

Preparation time about 30 minutes

Cooking time about 10 minutes

Serves 4

CULLEN SKINK

8 oz (225 g) smoked haddock or
    other smoked fish
1 onion, peeled and finely chopped
1 clove garlic, crushed (optional)
2 1/2 cups (21 fl oz, 600 ml) water
2 1/2 cups (21 fl oz, 600 ml) milk
salt and freshly ground black
    pepper
1–1 1/2 cups (8–12 oz, 225–350 g)
    mashed potato, hot
2 tablespoons (1 oz, 25 g) butter
2–3 teaspoons lemon juice
4 tablespoons cream
4 level tablespoons freshly chopped
    parsley

Put fish into a saucepan with onion, garlic and water. Bring to a boil, remove any scum, then cover and simmer gently for about 15 minutes until tender.

Remove fish from pan, remove and reserve skin and bones, and flake the flesh finely. Strain liquid and reserve the pieces of onion. Return liquid to the pan with skin and bones and simmer for a further 10–15 minutes.

Strain stock again and return 16 fl oz (450 ml) to saucepan with milk, flaked fish, onion and seasonings. Bring to a boil and simmer for 3 minutes. Gradually whisk in sufficient mashed potato to give your preferred consistency.

Stir in butter until melted. Sharpen to taste with lemon juice and seasonings. Add cream and most of the parsley and reheat gently.

Serve very hot, liberally sprinkled with remaining parsley and accompanied by hot crusty bread.

Preparation time about 40 minutes

Cooking time about 30 minutes

Serves 5–6

Note: The potatoes in this traditional Scottish soup must be mashed to very smooth before adding to avoid lumpiness. This soup can be sieved or pureed if preferred.

DU BARRY SOUP

2 oz (50 g) butter or margarine
1 large onion, peeled and finely
    chopped
1 small cauliflower, about
    1¹/₂–2 lb (675–900 g), trimmed
    and cut into rough florets
12 oz (350 g) potatoes, peeled and
    diced
2¹/₂ cups (20 fl oz, 600 ml) chicken
    or vegetable stock
salt and freshly ground black
    pepper
little freshly grated nutmeg
1 bay leaf
2 cups (16 fl oz, 475 ml) milk
1 tablespoon lemon juice
¹/₃ cup (5 fl oz, 150 ml) light
    (single) cream
2 level tablespoons freshly chopped
    chervil
fresh chervil leaves to garnish
toasted flaked almonds to garnish

Melt butter in a large saucepan and sauté onion very gently until soft but not browned, about 5 minutes.

Add cauliflower and potato to pan and continue to fry gently for 2–3 minutes.

Add stock, seasonings, nutmeg and bay leaf and bring to a boil. Cover and simmer for about 30 minutes until tender. Discard the bay leaf.

Sieve the soup or puree in a blender or food processor and return to a clean pan with milk and lemon juice to taste and simmer for 3–4 minutes.

Stir in cream and chopped chervil and reheat gently. Adjust the seasonings and serve sprinkled with fresh chervil leaves and toasted almonds.

Preparation time about 15 minutes

Cooking time about 45 minutes

Serves 6

Note: The soup may be frozen without the addition of cream or fresh chervil for up to 3 months.

FRITTERS

1/2 cup (4 oz, 100 g) all-purpose
  (plain) flour
salt and freshly ground black
  pepper
2 eggs
1 cup (8 fl oz, 200 ml) milk
1 lb (450 g) potatoes, boiled, peeled
  and cut into very small dice
7 oz (200 g) can corn kernels, well
  drained
6 scallions (shallots), trimmed and
  cut into narrow slanting slices
1 level tablespoon freshly chopped
  mixed herbs or 1 level teaspoon
  dried mixed herbs
oil for shallow-frying
watercress to garnish
crisp bacon and broiled (grilled)
  tomatoes to serve

Sift flour into a bowl with salt and pepper to taste. Make a well in the middle and add eggs and a little milk. Whisk to combine, gradually adding more milk as necessary to give a fairly thick, smooth batter.

Add potato to the batter with corn, onions and herbs, mixing well.

Heat about 1/2 inch (1 cm) oil in a frying pan and add large tablespoons of batter mixture to the oil. Cook for about 2 minutes each side until golden brown. Drain thoroughly on paper towels and keep warm while cooking the remaining fritters.

Serve the fritters garnished with watercress as a snack, or for a hearty breakfast with crisp bacon and broiled (grilled) tomatoes.

Preparation time about 15 minutes

Cooking time about 15 minutes

Makes about 12 fritters

GNOCCHI

1 lb (450 g) potato, mashed
salt and freshly ground black
    pepper
1¹/4 cups (6 oz, 175 g) all-purpose
    (plain) flour
1/4 level teaspoon grated or ground
    nutmeg
1 egg, beaten

Sauce:
1–2 tablespoons olive oil
1–2 cloves garlic, crushed
1 large onion, peeled and thinly
    sliced or finely chopped
15 oz (425 g) can tomatoes,
    chopped
1 level tablespoon freshly chopped
    basil or oregano
1 level tablespoon tomato puree
4 tablespoons water
good pinch of sugar
1/3 cup (2 oz, 50 g) freshly grated
    parmesan cheese
freshly chopped parsley to garnish

Mash potato to creamy. Gradually work in flour followed by plenty of salt and pepper, nutmeg and egg.

On a floured surface, knead dough until smooth, adding flour if sticky. Divide dough into 3 pieces and shape each piece into a sausage about 1 inch (2.5 cm) in diameter. Cut into slices, about 3/4 inch (2 cm) thick, and mark each with the prongs of a fork. Place gnocchi on a lightly floured paper towel. Leave covered while making sauce.

For the sauce: Heat oil in a saucepan and fry garlic and onion very gently until soft and just lightly browned. Add tomatoes, basil, tomato puree, water and sugar and bring to a boil. Simmer gently for about 10 minutes until thickened. Season to taste and keep warm.

Heat a large saucepan of salted water to boiling, then add gnocchi, about 10 at a time, and simmer gently, uncovered, for about 5 minutes or until they float to the surface. Remove with a slotted spoon; drain well. Place in a lightly oiled serving dish and keep warm. Repeat with the remaining gnocchi. Pour hot tomato sauce over gnocchi and sprinkle liberally with grated parmesan cheese and parsley.

Serve hot with extra parmesan cheese and plenty of freshly ground black pepper.

Preparation time about 25 minutes

Cooking time about 15 minutes

Serves 4

HASH BROWNS

2 lb (900 g) potatoes, peeled and
    coarsely grated
salt and freshly ground black
    pepper
1 medium onion, peeled and very
    finely chopped or grated
2 egg yolks
1/4–1/2 level teaspoon paprika or
    grated nutmeg
oil for frying
freshly chopped parsley to garnish

Squeeze excess moisture from grated potato with a clean cloth or paper towel to dry as much as possible.

Place potato in a bowl with seasonings to taste, onion, egg yolks, and paprika and mix very thoroughly. Divide mixture into 8 even portions.

Heat a shallow layer of oil in a frying pan. Shape each portion of potato mixture into a round, square or triangle and add to pan. Fry gently for about 2–3 minutes on each side until golden brown, pressing cakes into shape with a palette knife as they cook.

Transfer carefully to crumpled paper towel to drain. Keep warm while cooking the remainder.

Serve hot, sprinkled liberally with chopped parsley.

Preparation time about 10 minutes

Cooking time about 10 minutes

Serves 4 (makes 8)

Note: Hash browns are delicious served with fried foods for breakfast, as a vegetable accompaniment to chicken, fish, steak, or chops or on their own as a snack.

HERBED POTATO GRATIN

2 large eggplants (aubergines),
    about 1¹/₂–2 lb (675–900 g),
    trimmed
salt and freshly ground black
    pepper
2 tablespoons olive oil
2 onions, peeled and thinly sliced
2–4 cloves garlic, crushed
15 oz (425 g) can tomatoes,
    chopped
1 level tablespoon tomato puree
mild chili sauce, about 1–2
    teaspoons or to taste (optional)
2 level teaspoons freshly chopped
    oregano or 1 level teaspoon
    dried oregano
1¹/₂ lb (675 g) potatoes, peeled and
    sliced
4 oz (100 g) garlic sausage, thinly
    sliced or diced
2 beefsteak tomatoes or 4 large
    tomatoes, sliced
¹/₄ cup (2 fl oz, 60 ml) water
4 oz, 100 g mozzarella cheese,
    thinly sliced
2 level tablespoons grated
    parmesan cheese
2 level tablespoons breadcrumbs
fresh herbs to garnish

Cut eggplants lengthwise into slices about ¹/₃ inch (1 cm) thick. Sprinkle liberally with salt and leave for 30 minutes. Wash salt off and dry.

Heat oil in a pan and fry onion and garlic together until soft and just beginning to brown. Add canned tomatoes, tomato puree, chili sauce (if using), herbs and seasonings and bring to a boil. Cover and simmer gently for 10 minutes.

Preheat oven to moderate (350°F, 180°C, Gas Mark 4). Lightly grease a large ovenproof dish, arrange half the potato in base. Cover with half the eggplant followed by tomato and onion mixture. Place slices of garlic sausage over tomato then cover with remaining eggplant and then potato.

Season well and add a layer of tomato slices. Add water to the ovenproof dish. Cover with mozzarella. Mix parmesan cheese with breadcrumbs and sprinkle over the top. Cover with a lid or foil.

Cook in oven for about 1 hour or until tender. Remove lid, increase temperature to fairly hot (425°F, 220°C, Gas Mark 7) and return to oven for about 10 minutes; or place under a broiler (grill) to brown the cheese topping. Serve garnished with fresh herbs.

Preparation time about 20 minutes

Cooking time about 1 hour 10 minutes

Serves 4

HERBED POTATO PARCELS

2 oz (50 g) butter or margarine
1 clove garlic, crushed
1/4–1/2 level teaspoon crushed sea salt
freshly ground black pepper
1 level tablespoon freshly chopped parsley
1 level tablespoon freshly chopped rosemary or 1 level teaspoon dried rosemary, crumbled
1 level tablespoon snipped chives or scallion (shallot) tops
24 small potatoes (about 1 1/2 lb, 675 g), scrubbed or peeled as liked

Preheat oven to moderate (350°F, 180°C, Gas Mark 4).

Melt butter and add to a large bowl with garlic, sea salt, pepper, herbs and chives. Mix well. Add potatoes, tossing them in the mixture.

Arrange potatoes on a large sheet of non-stick parchment (baking paper) or place in a large non-stick parchment bag (greaseproof baking bag). Add remaining herbed butter from bowl.

Fold paper over so potatoes are not wrapped too tightly and fold around the edges, pressing firmly to make a sealed parcel. The parcel may be stapled if preferred; or simply twist the bag end and secure with a twist tie or string.

Stand carefully on a baking sheet and cook in oven for about 45 minutes.

Carefully transfer the parcel to a serving dish without tearing it, and take to the table.

Cut the parcel open just before serving and spoon potatoes from the bag.

Preparation time about 5 minutes

Cooking time 45 minutes

Serves 4

Note: If potatoes are to be served cold, cook by this method for only 40 minutes and leave the bag unopened until cool or cold.

INDIAN-STYLE POTATOES WITH SPINACH

2 lb (900 g) English spinach or 1 lb
  (450 g) frozen leaf spinach,
  thawed and well drained
2 tablespoons oil
1–2 onions, peeled and thinly
  sliced
2 cloves garlic, crushed
1½ level teaspoons black mustard
  seeds
1 level teaspoon turmeric
¼ level teaspoon chili powder
2 level teaspoons ground coriander
good pinch of ground ginger
1 lb (450 g) potatoes, peeled and
  thickly sliced or cut into cubes
⅔ cup (5 fl oz, 150 ml) water
salt and freshly ground black
  pepper

Drain any excess water from spinach, put into a saucepan without adding water and cook over a very gentle heat for 10–12 minutes or until tender. Drain well and cool. If using frozen spinach, cook over a gentle heat for about 5 minutes to remove as much water as possible and drain as above.

Remove as much liquid from spinach as possible, using a potato masher or by squeezing between clean kitchen cloth or paper towels. Chop spinach finely.

Heat oil in a large saucepan and fry onion and garlic gently for about 5 minutes or until just beginning to brown. Add mustard seeds and continue frying until they pop. Stir in turmeric and other spices and cook for a further minute. Add potatoes and water and bring to a boil. Season well, cover and simmer gently for about 10 minutes or until potato is almost tender. Add chopped spinach and continue to simmer gently for about 5 minutes, stirring occasionally, until potato is quite tender. If mixture becomes too dry, add a couple of tablespoons of hot water to prevent sticking.

Serve hot.

Preparation time about 20 minutes

Cooking time about 20 minutes

Serves 4

Note: If black mustard seeds are unavailable use yellow mustard seeds.

IRISH STEW

2¹/₂ lb (1.1 kg) lamb (middle neck or shoulder cut)
2 large onions, peeled and thinly sliced
8 oz (225 g) carrots, peeled and sliced
1¹/₂ lb (675 g) potatoes, peeled and sliced
salt and freshly ground black pepper
1 level tablespoon freshly chopped parsley
1¹/₂ level teaspoons freshly chopped thyme or mint
about 2 cups (16 fl oz, 450 ml) lamb, beef or vegetable stock or water
fresh herbs or mint to garnish

Preheat oven to 325°F (160°C, Gas Mark 3).

Cut lamb into manageable pieces, discarding any chips of bone and excess fat.

In a large ovenproof dish, arrange alternate layers of meat, onion, carrots and potato. Sprinkle with seasonings and herbs as you layer. Finish with a layer of potato arranged in overlapping slices.

Bring stock or water to a boil and add enough to the ovenproof dish to come about halfway up the layers. Cover tightly and cook in oven for 2¹/₂ hours or until the meat is almost tender.

Remove cover and increase oven temperature to moderately hot (375°F, 190°C, Gas Mark 5). Cook a further 30 minutes or until potato has browned on top and the meat and vegetables are very tender.

Garnish each portion with fresh herbs and serve accompanied by a green vegetable.

Preparation time about 10 minutes

Cooking time about 3 hours

Serves 4

Note: If liked, sprinkle 1 oz (25 g) pearl barley over the first layer of meat to thicken the juices a little.

LYONNAISE POTATOES

2 lb (900 g) potatoes in their skins, scrubbed

3–4 tablespoons olive or sunflower oil

2 large onions, peeled and thinly sliced

1–2 cloves garlic, crushed (optional)

6–8 streaky bacon slices, rinded and chopped

salt and freshly ground black pepper

2 level tablespoons freshly chopped mixed herbs or mint or 1 level tablespoon dried mixed herbs or mint

Cook potatoes in boiling salted water for about 15 minutes or until nearly tender. Drain, cool a little, peel and cut into even slices or cubes of about 3/4 inch (2 cm).

Heat half the oil in a pan and fry onions and garlic (if using) until golden brown. Remove from pan and keep warm.

Fry bacon in the same oil until crisp. Drain and add to onions.

Heat remaining oil in pan, add potatoes and cook until well browned. Return onions and bacon to pan with plenty of seasoning and continue to cook for a few minutes more. Stir in most of the herbs and turn into a serving dish.

Sprinkle with remaining herbs and serve hot.

Preparation time about 10 minutes

Cooking time about 20 minutes

Serves 4

Variation: Thin strips of prosciutto may be added instead of bacon when the onions are combined with potatoes.

MARSALA POTATOES

2 lb (900 g) new potatoes in their
   skins, scrubbed
oil for deep-frying
1 in (2.5 cm) piece fresh root
   ginger, peeled and chopped
4 cloves garlic, crushed
2 onions, peeled and chopped
2 level teaspoons ground coriander
1¹/₂ level teaspoons ground cumin
2 level teaspoons garam marsala
1–2 tablespoons water
2–3 tablespoons vegetable or
   sunflower oil
¹/₂ small green chili, seeded and
   chopped
1 level teaspoon salt
2 cups (10 fl oz, 300 ml) plain
   (natural) yogurt
2–3 level tablespoons freshly
   chopped cilantro (fresh
   coriander leaves)

Cut potatoes into pieces of about 1 inch (2.5 cm); if small, some of the potatoes may be left whole. Dry thoroughly.

Heat oil to 350°F (180°C) in a pan suitable for deep-frying and fry the potatoes in batches for about 10 minutes until golden brown and cooked through. Remove and drain thoroughly on paper towel. Alternatively, put potato pieces into a microwave-proof dish with 2 tablespoons water, cover and cook in a microwave oven on maximum (100%) for 9 minutes, giving a stir halfway through the cooking.

Put ginger, garlic and onions into a blender or food processor and process until well blended. Add coriander, cumin and garam marsala and process until well blended, adding a little water if necessary to make a paste.

Heat vegetable oil in a large pan and fry chili gently for a few minutes, add marsala paste and cook for a few minutes more, stirring frequently. Gradually add salt and yogurt and heat gently, stirring continuously. Add cooked potato and toss thoroughly over heat for several minutes until piping hot.

Adjust seasonings and either stir in chopped cilantro or turn potato into a dish and serve sprinkled liberally with cilantro.

Preparation time about 20 minutes

Cooking time about 15 minutes

Serves 4

Note: This dish makes a very interesting accompaniment to any meat or poultry dish.

NEW POTATOES WITH SOUR CREAM AND CAVIAR

1 lb (450 g) salad potatoes or tiny
    new potatoes in their skins,
    scrubbed
salt and freshly ground black
    pepper
3 oz (75 g) light soft cream cheese
6 tablespoons sour cream
2 level tablespoons red lumpfish
    roe (mock caviar in a jar)
2 level tablespoons black lumpfish
    roe (mock caviar in a jar)
mixed radicchio and lollo rosso
    lettuce (brown lettuce) leaves
tiny sprigs of mint or continental
    parsley

Cook potatoes in boiling salted water for about 10–15 minutes until tender, drain and leave until cold. Chill until required.

Cut any potatoes larger than a walnut in half and cut a small slice from the base of each potato so it will stand flat.

Combine cream cheese and sour cream, mix until smooth and spoon a little on top of each potato, or put into a piping bag fitted with a large star vegetable nozzle and pipe a small whirl onto each one.

Place a small teaspoonful of caviar in the middle of the cream on each potato, alternating with black and red lumpfish.

On a serving platter, make a bed of mixed radicchio and lollo rosso lettuce leaves and arrange potatoes on platter.

Garnish each with a tiny sprig of mint or parsley.

Preparation time about 20 minutes

Cooking time 10–15 minutes

Makes 20–25

Note: Ideal as a starter or to serve as a cocktail snack, the red and black lumpfish roe make this a very attractive dish. If red lumpfish roe is unavailable use black caviar and garnish with cherry tomatoes for added appeal.

OLIVE POTATO BREAD

6 oz (175 g) mashed or sieved
  potatoes
2 tablespoons (1 oz, 25 g) butter or
  margarine
4 cups (1 lb, 450 g) baker's flour,
  sifted
salt
1 tablespoon (1/2 oz, 15 g) fresh
  yeast or 1 1/2 level teaspoons
  dried yeast plus 1 level teaspoon
  sugar
2/3 cup (5 fl oz, 150 ml) warm
  milk, about 110°F (43°C)
2/3 cup (5 fl oz, 150 ml) warm
  water, about 110°F (43°C)
20 pitted black olives, thinly sliced

Note: The best results are achieved with freshly boiled and sieved potatoes.

Variation: For cheese and potato bread, omit olives and add 4 oz (100 g) finely grated mature cheddar or parmesan cheese at the knocking back stage.

Weigh 4 oz (100 g) of mashed potato and beat in butter, followed by flour and 1 level teaspoon salt. Blend fresh yeast with milk. If using dried yeast, dissolve sugar in milk, then sprinkle yeast over and leave in a warm place for about 10 minutes until frothy.

Add yeast liquid and warm water to dry ingredients and mix to form a fairly firm dough. Turn onto a floured surface and knead until smooth and even — about 10 minutes by hand or 3–4 minutes in an electric mixer fitted with a dough hook. Shape into a ball, place in an oiled plastic bag and put to rise in a warm place until doubled in size.

Turn out dough (which will be rather soft), and knead until smooth, adding 2/3 of the sliced olives. Shape to fit a greased 2 lb (900 g) loaf tin or divide into 3 oz (75 g) pieces, shape into flattish rolls and place on greased baking sheets. Cover with greased plastic wrap and put to prove in a warm place until the dough reaches the top of the tin or the rolls double in size. Remove wrap and sprinkle with the remaining olives.

Preheat oven to 425°F (220°C, Gas Mark 7). Bake about 40 minutes for the loaf (or until the base of the loaf sounds hollow when tapped) or 15–20 minutes for the rolls. Cool on a wire rack.

Preparation time about 25 minutes plus proving

Cooking time 40–45 minutes for loaf (15–20 minutes for rolls)

Makes 1 loaf or 6–8 rolls

PEPERONI PIZZA

6 oz (175 g) potatoes, peeled and
    diced
salt and freshly ground black
    pepper
2 tablespoons (1 oz, 25 g) butter or
    margarine
4 oz (100 g) self rising flour
1 tablespoon milk
2–3 tablespoons olive oil

Topping:
1 onion, peeled and thinly sliced
1–2 cloves garlic, crushed
2 oz (50 g) button mushrooms
    (champignons), sliced
2–3 oz (50–75 g) peperoni or
    salami, thinly sliced
2–3 large tomatoes, sliced
1 level teaspoon freshly chopped
    thyme or oregano or 1/2 level
    teaspoon dried thyme or
    oregano
2 oz (50 g) mozzarella cheese,
    sliced
1/2 cup (2 oz, 50 g) grated mature
    cheddar cheese

Cook potato in boiling salted water for 10–15 minutes
until tender or place in a microwave-proof dish with
3 tablespoons water and a pinch of salt, cover and cook in
microwave oven on maximum (100%) for 9 minutes,
stirring halfway through. Drain.

Thoroughly mash potato or puree in a blender or food
processor. Add butter and seasonings to taste and mash until
smooth. Gradually work in flour and milk to give a fairly
stiff dough. On a floured surface, carefully roll out to a
round about 8 inches (20 cm) in diameter.

Heat a tablespoon of oil in a heavy-based, non-stick frying
pan and fry pizza base gently for 7–8 minutes or until
underside is well browned.

Meanwhile heat remaining oil in a pan and fry onion and
garlic until beginning to brown. Add mushrooms and fry
for a few minutes longer.

Spoon onion mixture over base, and cover with peperoni,
tomatoes and herbs. Place slices of mozzarella on top and
sprinkle with grated cheddar. Place under a moderate broiler
(grill) and cook until cheese is melted and browned. Cut
into wedges and serve hot with a salad.

Preparation time about 20 minutes

Cooking time about 20 minutes

Serves 4

PICADILLO

1 lb (450 g) lean ground (minced)
    beef, or a mixture of beef and
    pork
2 onions, peeled and thinly sliced
2–3 cloves garlic, crushed
1 large carrot, peeled and chopped
    or coarsely grated
15 oz can (425 g) chopped
    tomatoes with herbs
2 level tablespoons tomato puree
1–2 tablespoons sweet chili sauce
3 oz (75 g) seedless raisins
3/4 cup (6 fl oz, 175 ml) red wine
3/4 cup (6 fl oz, 175 ml) stock or
    water
1/2 level teaspoon ground
    cinnamon
large pinch of ground allspice
salt and freshly ground black
    pepper
1 1/2 lb (675 g) sweet potato, peeled
    and cubed to about 3/4 in (2 cm)
    dice
1/3 cup (1 1/2 oz, 40 g) almonds,
    blanched and toasted, to
    garnish

Put meat into a heavy-based saucepan with onion, garlic and
carrot and cook gently for about 10 minutes, stirring from
time to time, until well sealed. Add chopped tomatoes,
tomato puree, chili sauce, raisins, wine, stock, spices and
seasonings and bring to a boil. Cover and simmer gently for
10 minutes.

Add sweet potato to pan, mixing well. Cover and simmer
for about 20 minutes or until potato is tender and the sauce
has thickened.

Adjust seasonings to taste and serve picadillo topped with
toasted almonds. A green salad or a green vegetable make a
good accompaniment.

Preparation time about 20 minutes

Cooking time about 30 minutes

Serves 4

PICKLED POTATO SALAD

12 oz (350 g) potatoes, peeled
salt and freshly ground black
    pepper
2 tablespoons French dressing
    (see page 58)
4 tablespoons plain (natural)
    yogurt
grated rind 1/2 lemon
12 oz (350 g) cauliflower, cut into
    florets
1 small purple (Spanish) onion,
    peeled and thinly sliced
4 large gherkins, drained and cut
    into narrow slanting slices
2 level tablespoons capers
few leaves broadleaf (curly)
    endive or radicchio
8 oz (250 g) cooked beets
    (beetroot), diced
4 oz (100 g) smoked salmon or
    pickled herring fillets, cut into
    thin strips

Cook potatoes in boiling salted water for about 10–15 minutes until just tender, drain, cool a little and cut into about 1/2 inch (1.5 cm) cubes. Place in a bowl.

Alternatively, cube potatoes, place in a microwave-proof dish with a pinch of salt and 3 tablespoons water, cover and cook in microwave oven on maximum (100%) for 9 minutes, giving a stir halfway through cooking.

Combine dressing, yogurt, lemon rind and seasonings to taste. Pour over potatoes and turn them evenly in the dressing. Leave to cool.

Blanch cauliflower in boiling salted water for 2 minutes. Drain, rinse under cold water and drain again.

Add cauliflower, onion, gherkins and capers to potato and toss together lightly.

Present the salad on a flat serving platter, surrounded with pieces of curly endive or radicchio, top with beet and arrange strips of smoked salmon over the middle.

Serve with fresh rustic bread or rolls.

Preparation time about 25 minutes

Cooking time about 10 minutes

Serves 4

Variation: Try strips of salami, smoked pork, smoked breast of chicken or duck instead of fish.

POTATO AND ARTICHOKE SALAD

1 lb (450 g) baby salad potatoes
   (pink variety if possible) in their
   skins or 1 1/4 lb (550 g) potatoes
   in their skins, scrubbed
salt and freshly ground black
   pepper
4 tablespoons French dressing (see
   below)
2 tablespoons plain (natural)
   yogurt
1 clove garlic, crushed
15 oz (425 g) can artichoke hearts,
   drained and cut in half or
   quartered
6 scallions (shallots), trimmed and
   cut into thin slanting slices
1/2 cucumber, about 3 in (7.5 cm),
   cut into 1 1/2 in (4 cm) narrow
   sticks
16 pitted black olives, halved
1 level tablespoon freshly chopped
   mint
mint sprigs to garnish

Cook potatoes in boiling salted water until just tender —
10 minutes for salad or 15–20 minutes for large — then
drain. Alternatively, place pricked potatoes on a paper towel
in a microwave and cook on maximum (100%) for 6
minutes; turn and cook a further 7 minutes or until tender.

Place salad potatoes in a bowl, cutting any large ones in half.
If using large potatoes, cool a little, make a cut in the skins
and peel. Cut the flesh into large dice and place in a bowl.

Whisk dressing, yogurt and garlic until completely
emulsified and pour over potato while still hot. Turn evenly
in dressing and leave until cold.

Add artichokes, onions, cucumber sticks and olives to bowl.
Season well, add chopped mint and mix thoroughly. Serve
on a bed of lettuce and garnish with fresh mint.

Preparation time about 30 minutes

Cooking time about 10 minutes

Serves 4

Note: For a homemade French dressing, put the following
ingredients into a jar with a good seal: 2/3 cup (5 fl oz,
150 ml) vegetable or sunflower oil, 3 tablespoons olive oil,
salt and freshly ground black pepper, 1–2 crushed cloves of
garlic, 1 level teaspoon dry (English) mustard, 1/2–1 level
teaspoon sugar, 1 tablespoon lemon juice, and 1 tablespoon
wine vinegar. Shake until completely emulsified. Shake again
immediately before use. Keeps about 2 weeks in refrigerator.

POTATO AND WATERCRESS SOUP

2 oz (50 g) butter or margarine
8 scallions (shallots), trimmed and
  sliced
12 oz (350 g) potatoes, peeled and
  diced
2 bunches watercress, trimmed
  and roughly chopped
3 cups (24 fl oz, 750 ml) chicken or
  vegetable stock
salt and freshly ground black
  pepper
1/2 teaspoon Worcestershire sauce
2 teaspoons lemon juice
1 1/4 cups (10 fl oz, 300 ml) milk
6 tablespoons light (single) cream
6 tablespoons plain (natural)
  yogurt
watercress sprigs to garnish

Melt butter in a large saucepan and sauté onions and potato gently for a few minutes without browning.

Add watercress to pan and toss. Add stock, seasonings, Worcestershire sauce and lemon juice and bring to a boil. Cover and simmer gently for about 30 minutes until tender.

Cool slightly and either sieve the soup or puree in a blender or food processor and return to a clean pan. Stir in milk and bring back to a boil for about 1 minute.

Thoroughly blend cream and yogurt, and add about half to the soup. Reheat gently and adjust seasonings.

Serve each portion with a spoonful of the remaining cream and yogurt mixture swirled through it and topped with watercress sprigs.

Preparation time 15–20 minutes

Cooking time about 40 minutes

Serves 6

Note: Without the addition of cream and yogurt, this soup may be frozen for up to 3 months.

Variation: For a chilled soup, cool and chill thoroughly after pureeing. Stir in the cream and yogurt before serving.

POTATO BEIGNETS AND CHILI DIP

*1 lb (450 g) potatoes, peeled and
diced*
*salt and freshly ground black
pepper*
3 oz (75 g) butter or margarine
2/3 cup (5 fl oz, 150 ml) water
*1/2 cup (2 1/2 oz, 65 g) all-purpose
(plain) flour, sifted*
2 eggs, beaten
additional flour for coating
*1 cup (4 oz, 100 g) fresh or dried
breadcrumbs*
oil for deep-frying
Chili dip:
*3 oz (75 g) low-fat soft cream
cheese*
*2–3 scallions (shallots), trimmed
and finely chopped*
*1–2 level tablespoons freshly
chopped parsley*
1 tablespoon sweet chili sauce
*2–3 tablespoons plain (natural)
yogurt, fromage frais or sour
cream*

Cook potatoes in a saucepan of boiling salted water for about 15 minutes until tender.

Meanwhile, melt 2 oz (50 g) butter in a pan. Add water and bring to a boil. Add flour and beat until choux mixture is smooth and forms a ball, leaving the sides of the pan clean. Remove from heat and leave to cool for a few minutes.

Cream potato with remaining 1 oz (25 g) butter and season lightly. Beat half the egg into choux mixture until smooth and then beat in the potato.

Place in a piping bag, if using, fitted with a large plain nozzle. Heat oil in a pan for deep-frying until just smoking and pipe in mixture to form 1 inch (2.5 cm) pieces. Fry for 3–4 minutes, turning as necessary until well puffed up and golden brown. Drain on paper towels and keep warm while cooking the remainder. Alternatively, form mixture into balls, roll in flour, dip in remaining egg, and coat in breadcrumbs. Place on a well-greased baking sheet and cook in a moderately hot oven (400°F, 200°C, Gas Mark 6) for about 20 minutes or until well risen and golden brown.

Chili dip: Combine all ingredients, blending well. Season to taste and place in a bowl surrounded by beignets.

Serve warm to accompany a meal or as a snack with dip.

Preparation time about 25 minutes

Cooking time about 15 minutes

Serves 4–6

POTATO CREPES WITH SALMON MOUSSE

*1/2 lb (225 g) potatoes in their
    skins, scrubbed*
*salt and freshly ground black
    pepper*
4 tablespoons hot milk
*1/3 cup (1 1/2 oz, 40 g) all-purpose
    (plain) flour, sifted*
2 eggs
1 egg white
*2 tablespoons light (single) cream
    or plain (natural) yogurt*
butter or oil for frying

Salmon mousse:
*4 oz (100 g) smoked salmon pieces
    (sandwich pieces or trimmings)*
*1 level tablespoon finely chopped
    onion*
1 clove garlic, crushed
3 oz (75 g) low-fat cream cheese
1–2 teaspoons lemon juice
*2 tablespoons light (single) cream
    or plain (natural) yogurt*
black olives to garnish
tomato slices to garnish
*green onion (scallion) tassels to
    garnish*

Cook potatoes in salted water for about 15–20 minutes until tender, drain, cool slightly, and peel. Mash potatoes until smooth, adding milk. Let cool.

Put mashed potato into a blender or food processor with flour and plenty of seasoning and blend to smooth. Add eggs and egg white, each separately, followed by cream and blend to smooth. Remove from blender and leave to stand while making the mousse.

For the mousse: Put smoked salmon pieces into a blender or food processor with onion and garlic and puree until smooth. Add cream cheese, lemon juice and cream and process until smooth but still very thick. Season to taste with a little salt and plenty of pepper.

To cook the crepes: Melt a little butter in a heavy-based frying pan and put about 2 tablespoons of potato mixture into pan. Cook for about 2 minutes until the underside is golden brown, turn carefully and continue for a minute more until cooked through and crisp. Transfer to a serving dish and keep warm while cooking the remainder.

Place each crepe on a plate and add a spoonful of smoked salmon mousse to the middle of each. Garnish with black olives and tomato slices and complete with an onion tassel.

Preparation time about 30 minutes

Cooking time about 15 minutes

Makes 8 (serves 4 for a light meal or 8 for a starter)

POTATO GALETTE

2¹/4 lb (1 kg) potatoes, peeled and
    cubed
3 tablespoons milk
salt and freshly ground black
    pepper
3 tablespoons olive oil
1 large onion, peeled and thinly
    sliced
2 cloves garlic, crushed
4 oz (100 g) carrots, peeled and
    coarsely grated or 1–2 leeks,
    trimmed and thinly sliced
¹/2 level teaspoon ground
    coriander
1–2 level tablespoons freshly
    chopped basil or 1 level
    teaspoon dried basil
fresh basil leaves to garnish

Place potato in a microwave-proof dish with 3 tablespoons milk, salt and pepper and cover with plastic wrap (cling film). Make a slit in the plastic and cook in a microwave oven on maximum (100%) for 9 minutes, giving a stir halfway through. Alternatively, cook in boiling salted water for about 10 minutes until tender.

Mash microwaved potatoes as they are; or drain and mash boiled potatoes, adding milk and seasonings.

Meanwhile, heat half the oil in a pan and fry onions and garlic for 3–4 minutes until soft. Add carrot and cook for 2–3 minutes.

In a bowl, combine onion mixture with potato, coriander and basil and mix well.

Heat remaining oil in a non-stick frying pan and add potato mixture, flattening it out with a spatula. Cook over a gentle heat until just browned underneath then place under a moderate broiler (grill) until the top is evenly browned.

Serve cut into quarters and garnished with fresh basil.

Preparation time about 25 minutes

Cooking time about 15 minutes

Serves 4

Note: Make individual galettes by dividing the mixture into 4 round cakes and finishing as above.

POTATO NIÇOISE

1 lb (450 g) pink salad potatoes in
    their skins, scrubbed
salt and freshly ground black
    pepper
4–6 tablespoons French dressing
    (see page 58)
2 level teaspoons freshly chopped
    fennel or parsley
6 oz (175 g) green (French) beans,
    trimmed and halved
1/2 red bell pepper (capsicum),
    seeded and cut into narrow
    strips
4 oz (100 g) raw carrots, peeled
    and cut into narrow sticks
7 oz (200 g) can tuna fish in brine,
    drained and roughly flaked
1 small onion, peeled and very
    thinly sliced
1 small crisp lettuce (cos or little
    gem)
2 hard-cooked (hard-boiled) eggs,
    quartered
few black olives (optional)
1 can anchovy fillets, drained
    (optional)

Place potatoes in a microwave-proof bowl with 3 tablespoons water and a little salt, cover and cook in a microwave oven on maximum (100%) for 10 minutes, then leave to partially cool; or cook in boiling salted water for 10–15 minutes until just tender and drain.

Cut potatoes into even-sized pieces about 3/4 inch (2 cm) and place in a bowl with dressing and fennel. Toss to combine and leave until cold.

Cook French beans in boiling salted water for about 4 minutes until tender but still crisp. Drain, run under cold water to cool and drain again. Add to the salad with bell pepper, carrot, tuna and onion and toss lightly to combine.

Arrange lettuce leaves in a shallow dish and spoon on niçoise. Top with quartered eggs, black olives and anchovy fillets, if using, and serve with plenty of crusty bread.

Preparation time 25 minutes

Cooking time 15 minutes

Serves 4

Variations: Chopped raw Florence fennel may be added to the salad or try snow peas (mange tout) or broad beans in place of French beans.

Potato Skins with Three Dips

6 medium potatoes (about 2 lb, 900 g) in their skins, scrubbed and pricked all over with a fork
4 tablespoons oil or 2 oz (50 g) butter or margarine, melted
salt and freshly ground black pepper

Avocado dip:
1 ripe avocado
1 teaspoon lemon juice
3 oz (75 g) low-fat cream cheese
2 scallions (shallots), trimmed and finely chopped
2 level teaspoons freshly chopped mint (optional)

Garlic cheese dip:
4 oz (100 g) cream cheese
3 oz (75 g) blue cheese
2 cloves garlic, crushed
2–3 tablespoons plain (natural) yogurt

Smoked salmon dip:
4 oz (100 g) smoked salmon pieces
1 teaspoon lemon juice
4 tablespoons fromage frais or plain (natural) yogurt
1 level teaspoon freshly chopped dill or tarragon

Bake potatoes in a fairly hot oven (425°F, 220°C, Gas Mark 7) for 1–1¼ hours until tender, or place on a paper towel in a microwave oven and cook on maximum (100%) for 6 minutes, turn and cook 7 minutes or until tender. Halve each potato and scoop out most of the flesh, leaving about ½ inch (5 mm) on the skin. Cut each half into 3 or 4 wedges, using kitchen shears or a knife. Place skins on a baking sheet, brush inside each with oil and season.

Cook in a fairly hot oven (425°F, 220°C, Gas Mark 7) for about 20 minutes or until lightly browned and crisp; alternatively place under a moderate broiler (grill).

For avocado dip: Quarter, peel and seed avocado. Puree in a blender or food processor with lemon juice, cheese, onions and seasonings to taste. Add mint, if liked, and serve.

For garlic cheese dip: Combine ingredients in a blender or food processor and puree. Season to taste and serve.

For smoked salmon dip: In a blender or food processor, puree salmon pieces and lemon juice until smooth. Combine with sufficient fromage frais to give required consistency. Season to taste, stir in herbs, and serve.

Serve dips on a large platter surrounded by hot potato skins.

Preparation time about 25 minutes

Cooking time about 1½ hours

Serves 4

POTATO WAFFLES

1¹/₂ lb (675 g) potatoes, peeled and
   diced

2 oz (50 g) butter or margarine

salt and freshly ground black
   pepper

good pinch of freshly grated or
   ground nutmeg

4–6 tablespoons milk

3 oz (75 g) all-purpose (plain) flour

³/₄ level teaspoon baking powder

additional butter or oil for
   greasing

Boil potatoes in salted water for about 10 minutes until tender; or place in a microwave-proof dish with salt and 3 tablespoons water, cover and cook in a microwave oven on maximum (100%) for 10 minutes.

Drain and mash or sieve, adding butter, salt, pepper, nutmeg and enough milk to achieve a very smooth consisitency. Sift together flour and baking powder, and beat into the potato mixture, which should now be firm enough to shape into cakes.

Heat a waffle iron following the manufacturer's instructions and brush with melted butter before cooking each waffle.

Fill waffle iron with sufficient potato mixture, close and cook until the waffles are golden and crisp. Remove carefully and keep warm while cooking remaining waffles.

Serve hot as an accompaniment to any meal of the day, breakfast, lunch, dinner, supper, or just as a snack.

Preparation time about 25 minutes

Cooking time 10–20 minutes

Makes about 8 waffles

Note: If you don't have a waffle iron, divide mixture into 8 portions and shape into round cakes. Cook slowly in a frying pan in about ¹/₂ inch (5 mm) hot oil until golden brown on both sides.

POTATO WEDGES WITH CHILI BEEF

6 potatoes, about 6 oz (175 g) each
    or 2–3 sweet potatoes, about
    2^1/$_4$ lb (1 kg) total
2 tablespoons oil
salt and freshly ground black
    pepper
1 lb (450 g) lean ground (minced)
    beef
1 large onion, peeled and finely
    chopped
2 cloves garlic, crushed
1lb (450 g) tomatoes, peeled and
    sliced
2 level teaspoons freshly chopped
    basil or 1 level teaspoon dried
    basil
1 level tablespoon tomato puree
^{1}/$_2$ small red chili, seeded and
    chopped
4–6 tablespoons beef or vegetable
    stock or water
15 oz (425 g) can red kidney
    beans, drained
freshly chopped parsley or cilantro
    (fresh coriander leaves) to
    garnish

Preheat oven to moderately hot (400°F, 200°C, Gas Mark 6).

Cut each potato into six lengthwise wedges. If using long sweet potatoes, halve or cut into thirds before cutting into wedges. Brush each wedge with oil and sprinkle with salt. Stand on a baking sheet and cook in oven for about 40 minutes or until golden brown and cooked through. Both types of potato take the same cooking time.

Meanwhile, put beef into a heavy-based saucepan with onion and garlic but no added oil and cook gently for about 10 minutes, stirring frequently until well sealed. Add tomatoes, basil, tomato puree, chili, stock and seasonings and bring to a boil. Cover and simmer for about 15 minutes or until tender. Add beans and simmer, uncovered, for about 10 minutes until quite thick.

Serve wedges with chili beef spooned over or beside them for dipping and garnish the chili beef with chopped parsley or cilantro.

Preparation time about 15 minutes

Cooking time about 45 minutes

Serves 4

Note: Wedges are a great snack as they are or with a variety of dips (see page 70). For a simple but delicious treat, try sweet potato wedges with sour cream and sweet chili sauce.

POTATO, ONION AND TOMATO BAKE

2¼ lb (1 kg) potatoes, peeled
salt and freshly ground black
  pepper
2 tablespoons olive oil
8 oz (225 g) onions, peeled and
  thinly sliced
2–4 cloves garlic, crushed
3 large tomatoes, about 1 lb
  (450 g), thinly sliced
2 level tablespoons freshly chopped
  tarragon or 1 level tablespoon
  dried tarragon
6–8 oz (175–225 g) mature
  cheddar cheese, grated
fresh tarragon to garnish

Parboil potatoes in salted water for 8–10 minutes then drain well. Cool slightly and slice potatoes.

Heat oil in a pan and sauté onion and garlic gently for about 5–10 minutes until soft but barely browned.

Preheat oven to moderately hot (375°F, 190°C, Gas Mark 5).

Grease a large ovenproof dish and layer up, first with half the sliced potato then half the onion, 1 sliced tomato, half the tarragon and one third of the cheese and season well. Repeat layers, adding an extra layer of tomato and grated cheese. Cook uncovered in oven for about 1 hour until the cheese is well melted into other ingredients and browned on top. Garnish with tarragon and serve.

Preparation time about 20 minutes

Cooking time about 1 hour

Serves 4

Variation: Other herbs may be used in place of tarragon. You may like to replace half the potatoes with sweet potatoes.

POTATOES WITH CUMIN AND SESAME SEEDS

*2¹/₄ lb (1 kg) new potatoes in their
   skins, scrubbed*
*salt and freshly ground black
   pepper*
2 tablespoons olive oil
*2 large onions, about 12 oz (350 g),
   peeled and thinly sliced*
2 cloves garlic, crushed
2 level tablespoons mustard seeds
3 level tablespoons sesame seeds
2–3 level teaspoons ground cumin
*1 level tablespoon freshly chopped
   parsley to garnish*
*2 level tablespoons snipped chives
   to garnish*

Boil potatoes in salted water for about 10 minutes until almost tender; cool a little and slice or cut into large dice. Or, cook potatoes in microwave-proof dish with 3 tablespoons water, salt and pepper to taste for 9 minutes in a microwave oven on maximum (100%), stirring halfway through cooking, then cut as above.

Heat oil in a frying pan and fry onions and garlic gently until soft but not browned. Add mustard seeds, sesame seeds and cumin, and mix well. Add potato and continue to fry for about 5 minutes or until well browned all over and coated in seeds. Season to taste and turn into a serving dish.

Combine parsley and chives and sprinkle evenly over potato.

Preparation time about 15 minutes

Cooking time about 15 minutes

Serves 4

RED LENTIL AND POTATO SOUP

1¹/₂ cups (8 oz, 225 g) red lentils
6¹/₄ cups (50 fl oz, 1.5 l) vegetable
   stock or water
1 ham bone or knuckle or 6 oz
   (175 g) streaky bacon slices,
   rinded and chopped
1 large onion, peeled and chopped
1 clove garlic, crushed
2 carrots, peeled and finely
   chopped or coarsely grated
3–4 tomatoes, peeled and chopped
1 bay leaf
salt and freshly ground black
   pepper
12 oz (350 g) potatoes, peeled and
   chopped
2 tablespoons wine vinegar
freshly chopped parsley to garnish
fried croutons to garnish (see note)

Wash lentils and place in a large saucepan with stock, ham bone, onion, garlic, carrot, tomato, bay leaf and seasonings. Bring to a boil, remove any scum from the surface, cover and simmer gently for about 1 hour or until the lentils are tender.

Discard bay leaf and remove ham bone, if used. If preferred, the soup may be sieved or pureed at this stage. Any trimmings may be removed from the ham bone, finely chopped and returned to the soup.

Add potato and vinegar and continue to simmer for about 20 minutes until potato is tender.

Adjust the seasonings and serve very hot, sprinkled liberally with chopped parsley and fried croutons.

Preparation time about 15 minutes

Cooking time about 1 hour 20 minutes

Serves 6

Note: For fried croutons, remove crusts from 3–4 slices bread (white or brown) and dice roughly. Heat about 1 inch (2.5 cm) oil in a frying pan, adding garlic, if liked. Add the bread and fry for 3–4 minutes, turning as necessary until golden brown. Discard garlic and drain croutons on paper towels. Store in an airtight container for up to 5 days.

This soup may be frozen, without croutons, for about 2 months.

ROSTI

2 tablespoons oil

1 large onion, peeled and chopped

1 large leek, trimmed and thinly
sliced

8 oz (225 g) carrots, peeled and
coarsely grated

1¹/₂ lb (675 g) potatoes, peeled and
coarsely grated

salt and freshly ground black
pepper

¹/₂ level teaspoon ground
coriander

about ¹/₃ cup (1¹/₂–2 oz, 40–50 g)
mature cheddar cheese, grated
(optional)

Heat 1 tablespoon of oil in a frying pan and fry onion and leek gently for about 5 minutes until soft but not browned. Turn into a bowl. Add carrot, potato, seasonings and coriander and mix well.

Heat remaining oil in pan and add potato mixture. Cook gently for about 5 minutes, stirring occasionally, then flatten down to form a cake. Continue for about 8–10 minutes until the cake has browned underneath and vegetables are almost cooked. Loosen from time to time with a spatula so the potato cake does not stick.

Sprinkle the top with cheese (if using) and put under a moderate broiler (grill) until lightly browned. Serve hot, cut into wedges.

Preparation time about 20 minutes

Cooking time about 20 minutes

Serves 4

Variation: Try mixing other vegetables with the potatoes in this recipe; you could use grated zucchini (courgettes), parsnips, celeriac or fennel.

SCALLOPED POTATOES

2¹/₂ lb (1 kg) potatoes, peeled and
    thinly sliced
2 onions, peeled and finely
    chopped
salt and freshly ground black
    pepper
1–2 cloves garlic, crushed
1 level tablespoon freshly chopped
    tarragon or dill or 1 level
    teaspoon dried tarragon or dill
1¹/₄ cups (10 fl oz, 300 ml) chicken,
    beef or vegetable stock or milk
    or light (single) cream or ²/₃ cup
    (5 fl oz, 150 ml) each stock and
    dry white wine
1 tablespoon (¹/₂ oz, 15 g) butter
    or margarine, melted
2 oz (50 g) mature cheddar or
    gouda cheese, grated
chopped mixed herbs to garnish

Preheat oven to moderately hot (400°F, 200°C, Gas Mark 6).

Arrange a layer of one third of the sliced potatoes in a well-greased ovenproof dish and sprinkle with half the onions. Season well and sprinkle with garlic and half the herbs.

Add another layer of potato, onion, seasonings and herbs and finish with a final potato layer, arranging slices in an attractive pattern.

Heat stock to just below boiling point and pour over potato. Brush the top layer with melted butter. Cover ovenproof dish and cook in oven for 1 hour.

Remove cover and sprinkle with cheese. Return to the oven, uncovered, for a further 30–45 minutes until well-browned on top and tender throughout.

Serve hot, sprinkled with chopped mixed herbs.

Preparation time about 20 minutes

Cooking time 1¹/₂–1³/₄ hours

Serves 4–6

Note: Keep this dish simple by using stock or transform it into elegant dinner party fare using cream.

Variations: Add 4 oz (100 g) diced bacon, diced smoked salmon pieces, salami or garlic sausage or sliced button mushrooms (champignons) with the herbs.

SHEPHERD'S PIE

1¹/₂ lb (675 g) ground (minced) beef or lamb, or a mixture of the two
1 large onion, peeled and finely chopped
1–2 cloves garlic, crushed
2 sticks celery, finely chopped
2 carrots, peeled and finely chopped or coarsely grated
8 oz (225 g) can peeled tomatoes, chopped
2–3 level teaspoons freshly chopped oregano or 1 teaspoon dried oregano
salt and freshly ground black pepper
1 teaspoon Worcestershire sauce
2 lb (900 g) potatoes, peeled and cubed
3 tablespoons (1¹/₂ oz, 40 g) butter or margarine
2–3 tablespoons milk
freshly chopped parsley to garnish

Preheat oven to moderately hot (400°F, 200°C, Gas Mark 6).

Place meat in a saucepan with onion, garlic, celery and carrot and cook gently for about 10 minutes over a gentle heat, stirring frequently until well sealed and almost cooked.

Add tomato, oregano, seasonings, Worcestershire sauce and 4 tablespoons water and simmer for 15 minutes until quite tender. Adjust seasonings, put in an ovenproof dish or divide between four individual ovenproof dishes.

Meanwhile, cook potato in boiling salted water for about 15 minutes until tender; or place in a microwave-proof dish with salt and 3 tablespoons water. Cover and cook in microwave oven on maximum (100%) for 9 minutes, stirring halfway through cooking.

Mash potato to smooth or process in a blender or food processor adding butter and milk until creamy.

Place in a piping bag fitted with a large vegetable star nozzle and pipe evenly over meat mixture or spread an even layer over the meat and fork up.

Cook in oven for 30–40 minutes or until the top is golden brown and the meat is piping hot.

Sprinkle with chopped parsley and serve.

Preparation time about 25 minutes

Cooking time about 40 minutes

Serves 4

SMOKY FISH CAKES

12 oz (350 g) smoked fish fillet
(smoked haddock, mackerel,
cod or similar fish) or 4 oz
(100 g) smoked salmon pieces
and 8 oz (225 g) white fish
fillets
2/3 cup (5 fl oz ,150 ml) milk
salt and freshly ground black
pepper
1 1/2 lb (675 g) potatoes, peeled
2 tablespoons (1 oz, 30 g) butter or
margarine
2 hard-cooked (hard-boiled) eggs,
chopped
2 level tablespoons snipped chives
3 level tablespoons freshly chopped
parsley
1 egg, beaten
fresh or dried breadcrumbs for
coating
oil for shallow-frying
Sauce:
4 tablespoons mayonnaise
1 tablespoon tomato puree
1 teaspoon sweet chili sauce
2 tablespoons plain (natural) yogurt
parsley sprigs to garnish
lemon or lime wedges to garnish

Poach fish (except smoked salmon, if using) in milk with seasonings and a little water for about 10 minutes until tender. Drain and reserve poaching liquid. Remove any skin and bones from fish and finely flake flesh. Chop smoked salmon, if using, and mix with the poached white fish.

Cook potatoes in boiling salted water for about 10–15 minutes until tender; drain. Mash, adding butter, seasonings and 1–2 tablespoons of poaching liquid to give a smooth, creamy consistency.

Add fish, eggs, chives and parsley and mix until evenly blended. Divide mixture into 8 portions and shape into flat, round cakes. Dip in beaten egg and coat with breadcrumbs.

Heat about 1/2 inch (1.5 cm) oil in a frying pan and fry fish cakes for about 5 minutes each side until golden brown. Alternatively, place fish cakes on a well-greased baking sheet and cook in a fairly hot oven (400°F, 200°C, Gas Mark 6) for 25–30 minutes until golden.

For the sauce: Combine ingredients, add seasonings to taste, mix well and place in a small bowl.

Drain fish cakes on paper towels, garnish with fresh parsley and lemon or lime wedges and serve hot with sauce.

Preparation time about 20 minutes

Cooking time about 10 minutes

Serves 4

SPANISH OMELETTE

2–3 tablespoons olive oil

1 large onion, peeled and very
    thinly sliced

1–2 cloves garlic, crushed

1 zucchini (courgette), about 4 oz
    (100 g), trimmed and very
    thinly sliced

1 red bell pepper (capsicum),
    seeded and thinly sliced

6 eggs

2 egg whites

salt and freshly ground black
    pepper

1 level tablespoon freshly chopped
    mixed herbs (parsley, thyme
    and oregano)

2 boiled potatoes, about 10 oz
    (300 g), diced

1/3 cup (2 oz, 50 g) frozen peas,
    thawed

2 large tomatoes, peeled, seeded
    and chopped

1/3 cup (2 oz, 50 g) mature cheddar
    or parmesan cheese, grated
    (optional)

Heat about 1½ tablespoons of oil in a large heavy-based frying pan, add onion and garlic and fry gently for 3–4 minutes until soft. Add zucchini and bell pepper and cook for about 5 minutes, stirring from time to time, until tender.

Beat eggs and egg whites with plenty of seasonings and herbs. Add remaining oil to the frying pan and, when hot, pour in egg mixture. Stir well and sprinkle potato, peas and tomato over omelette. Cook gently for about 5 minutes or until omelette is set and browned underneath.

If liked, sprinkle the top with grated cheese and then place under a moderate broiler (grill) for about 4–5 minutes until golden brown.

Cut into quarters and serve hot or cold with salads.

Preparation time about 20 minutes

Cooking time about 20 minutes

Serves 4

Note: If entertaining, this omelette may be cut into small squares and served cold as a delicious appetiser.

STIR-FRIED POTATO AND BROCCOLI

2 lb (900 g) sweet potatoes, peeled,
   or new potatoes in their skins,
   scrubbed

salt and freshly ground black
   pepper

1 lb (450 g) broccoli, cut into small
   florets

1 tablespoon sesame oil

1 tablespoon sunflower oil

1 level teaspoon mustard seeds

3 sticks green celery, cut into
   narrow slanting slices

6 scallions (shallots), trimmed and
   cut into slanting slices

1–2 cloves garlic, crushed

1 red bell pepper (capsicum),
   seeded and thinly sliced

7 oz (200 g) can corn kernels,
   drained

1 tablespoon light soy sauce

2 tablespoons medium sherry

1 level teaspoon ground cumin

freshly steamed rice or noodles to
   serve

Cook potatoes in boiling salted water until barely tender. Drain, cool a little and cut into about $1/2$ inch (1.5 cm) cubes. Alternatively, cut potatoes into dice, place in a microwave-proof dish with 3 tablespoons water and a sprinkling of salt, cover and cook in a microwave oven on maximum (100%) for 8 minutes.

Blanch broccoli in boiling salted water for 2 minutes and drain thoroughly.

Heat oils to very hot in a wok or large heavy-based frying pan. Add mustard seeds, and fry until they begin to pop. Add celery, onion, garlic and pepper and stir-fry for 3–4 minutes.

Add potato, broccoli and corn and continue to cook, stirring frequently, for about 5 minutes until almost tender.

Add soy sauce, sherry, cumin and plenty of seasonings, stirring for 2–3 minutes until well coated.

Serve with freshly boiled rice or noodles.

Preparation time about 20 minutes

Cooking time about 15 minutes

Serves 4

Variation: Experiment with other ingredients such as chicken, fish, shrimp (prawns), hard-cooked (hard-boiled) eggs, French beans, snow peas (mange tout), sliced zucchini (courgettes) or whatever you may have available.

Sweet Potato Bake

1 red bell pepper (capsicum),
 halved and seeded
1¹/2 lb (675 g) sweet potatoes,
 peeled and thinly sliced
8 oz (225 g) zucchini (courgettes),
 trimmed and thinly sliced
salt and pepper
1–2 tablespoons olive oil
1 large onion, peeled and sliced
2 cloves garlic, crushed
1 large leek, trimmed and sliced
6 oz (175 g) carrots, peeled and cut
 into narrow sticks
4 oz (100 g) snow peas (mange
 tout), trimmed
4 tomatoes, peeled and sliced
 (optional)
¹/2 cup (2 oz, 50 g) breadcrumbs
2 level tablespoons freshly chopped
 mixed herbs or 1 level
 tablespoon dried mixed herbs
Sauce:
3 tablespoons (1¹/2 oz, 40 g) butter
 or margarine
¹/3 cup (1¹/2 oz, 40 g) all-purpose
 (plain) flour
1 level teaspoon mustard powder
2 cups (17 fl oz, 475 ml) skim milk

Place bell pepper skin-side upwards on a rack and cook under a moderate boiler (grill) until the skin chars. Cool a little, peel off skin and slice bell pepper.

Preheat oven to moderate (350°F, 180°C, Gas Mark 4).

Arrange one third of the potato in a layer in a greased ovenproof dish. Cover with bell pepper and zucchini, season well, then make another layer of potatoes.

Heat oil in a frying pan and fry onion, garlic and leek for 2–3 minutes until soft. Drain oil from onion mixture and spread it over potato layer, followed by carrot, snow peas and tomato, if using. Season and make a final layer of potato.

For the sauce: Melt butter in a pan, stir in flour and mustard and cook for 1–2 minutes. Gradually add milk, bring to a boil and simmer for a couple of minutes until thickened. Season to taste. Pour sauce over potatoes, cover ovenproof dish and cook in oven for 1¹/2 hours.

Combine breadcrumbs and herbs and sprinkle over potato bake. Return to a hot oven (400°F, 200°C, Gas Mark 6), uncovered, for 15–20 minutes until browned.

Serve hot as a main dish or accompaniment.

Preparation time about 20 minutes

Cooking time about 1³/4 hours

Serves 4–6

Note: use ordinary potatoes and vary ingredients, as liked.

SWEET POTATO CHOWDER

1 chicken carcass, raw or cooked or
    2–3 chicken stock cubes
5 cups (38 fl oz, 1.1 l) water
salt and freshly ground black
    pepper
1 bouquet garni (parsley, bay leaf
    and thyme in cheesecloth)
2 oz (50 g) butter or margarine
1 large onion, peeled and finely
    chopped
2 sticks celery, finely chopped
1/4 cup (1 oz, 25 g) all-purpose
    (plain) flour, sifted
2 level teaspoons tomato puree
1/2–1 level teaspoon medium curry
    powder (optional)
2–3 carrots, peeled and finely
    chopped or coarsely grated
11 oz (325 g) can corn kernels,
    drained
1 small red bell pepper (capsicum),
    seeded and chopped
12 oz (350 g) sweet potatoes,
    peeled and finely chopped
1 teaspoon Worcestershire sauce
4 tablespoons freshly chopped
    parsley

Break up chicken carcass, place in a large saucepan with water, seasonings, bouquet garni and bring to a boil. Remove any scum from surface, cover and simmer for about 1 hour. Strain off the stock, reserving about 4 1/2 cups (35 fl oz, 1 l).

Pick about 3 oz (75 g) of chicken trimmings from carcass and chop finely. Alternatively, combine 4 1/2 cups (35 fl oz, 1 l) water with 2–3 chicken stock cubes.

Melt butter in a large saucepan pan and sauté onion and celery gently until soft but not browned. Stir in flour, tomato puree and curry powder (if using), and cook for 1–2 minutes, then gradually add reserved stock and bring to a boil.

Add carrot, corn, bell pepper, sweet potatoes and any chopped chicken, together with seasonings and Worcestershire sauce and simmer gently for about 20 minutes or until tender and fairly thick. Adjust the seasonings and stir half the parsley into the chowder.

Serve very hot, sprinkled with remaining parsley and accompanied by hot crusty bread or rolls.

Preparation time 10–15 minutes

Cooking time 1 hour 40 minutes (40 minutes for stock cubes)

Serves 4–6

Note: This soup may be frozen for up to 2 months.

Variation: For a vegetarian soup, omit chicken and use vegetable stock.

TATTIE 'ASH

1 tablespoon oil
1 lb (450 g) fresh sausages
(farmhouse sausages)
2 large onions, peeled and thinly
sliced
2 cloves garlic, crushed
1 lb (450 g) small new potatoes or
salad potatoes in their skins,
scrubbed
2 large carrots, peeled and cut into
sticks
1 large leek, trimmed, sliced and
washed
4 oz (100 g) salami, diced
1 teaspoon Worcestershire sauce
2/3 cup (5 fl oz, 150 ml) cider
1 cup (8 fl oz, 250 ml) stock
salt and freshly ground black
pepper
1 level tablespoon mustard seeds
1 level tablespoon freshly chopped
thyme or 1 level teaspoon dried
thyme

Preheat oven to moderate (350°F, 180°C, Gas Mark 4).

Heat oil in a frying pan and fry sausages until well browned, or brown them under a medium broiler (grill). Drain off excess oil and cut each in half. Fry onion and garlic in the same oil until lightly browned. Transfer to an ovenproof dish with sausages, potatoes (which may be peeled if preferred), carrot, leek and salami and mix well.

Combine Worcestershire sauce, cider and stock in a saucepan and bring to a boil. Season well and add mustard seeds and herbs.

Pour sauce over the potato mixture, cover tightly and cook in oven for 45–60 minutes until tender. Adjust seasonings and serve with a green vegetable or salad.

Preparation time about 10 minutes

Cooking time 45–60 minutes

Serves 4

Note: If you prefer a casserole where the potatoes break up and mingle with the sauce, use 1½ lb (675 g) floury potatoes, peeled and cut into large dice and cook as above.

Variation: In place of salami, crisply fried bacon may be used.

TATTIE SCONES

12 oz (350 g) potatoes, peeled and
    roughly diced
salt and freshly ground black
    pepper
2 oz (50 g) butter or margarine
good grating of nutmeg
about 4 oz (100 g) all-purpose
    (plain) flour

Boil potatoes in salted water for about 15 minutes or until tender and drain thoroughly; or place in a microwave-proof dish with 3 tablespoons water and a pinch of salt, cover and cook in a microwave oven on maximum (100%) for 9 minutes, giving a stir halfway through cooking.

Mash potatoes evenly until smooth either by hand or in a blender or food processor. Beat in butter, seasonings and nutmeg to taste .

Work sufficient flour into potato to give a pliable dough that is not too dry or crumbly.

Turn onto a lightly floured surface, roll out to about 1/4 inch (5 mm) thickness and cut into 2 inch (5 cm) rounds or larger rounds which can be divided into 4, 6 or 8 wedges.

Lightly dust a griddle or heavy-based frying pan with flour and heat it to fairly hot 425°F (220 °C).

Prick scones all over with a fork and cook on griddle or in pan for 2–3 minutes each side until golden brown. Immediately wrap in a clean kitchen cloth or paper towels and leave on a wire rack while cooking the remainder.

Serve warm with lashings of butter.

Preparation time about 20 minutes

Cooking time about 15 minutes

Makes about 12

TOPPED AND FILLED
BAKED JACKET POTATOES

4 baking potatoes (8–12 oz,
225–350 g each) in their skins,
scrubbed and pricked all over
with a fork
little oil (optional)
salt and freshly ground black
pepper
Toppings:
butter (or sour cream or fromage
frais) with chopped chives (or
herbs of your choice)
grated cheese (or cream cheese)
with chopped scallions
(shallots),
baked beans with grated cheese,
tomato and chili sauce
Fillings:
crisp bacon and chives, chopped
flaked tuna, sour cream and
grated cheese
blue stilton cheese with chopped
chives,(or chopped thyme or
marjoram) and fromage frais
shrimp (prawns) with scallions
(shallots) and sour cream
fried onions and corn with crisp
bacon

For a shiny skin , rub potato skins with oil. Cook in a fairly hot oven (425°F, 220°C, Gas Mark 7) for 1¼ hours or until tender. Alternatively, place pricked potatoes on a paper towel in a microwave oven and cook on maximum (100%) for 6 minutes, turn and cook a further 7 minutes.

For topped baked potatoes: Cut a cross in the top of each potato and squeeze gently at its base to open out. Top with a knob of butter and sprinkle with chopped chives, or spoon your choice from suggested toppings over the potato flesh.

For filled baked potatoes: Cut the top off each potato and carefully scoop out most of the flesh. Mash potato flesh to smooth, adding a good knob of butter and seasoning to taste. Mix with your choice of suggested fillings. Carefully return filling to potatoes, piling up as necessary. Stand potatoes on a baking sheet and return to a hot oven for about 10 minutes or place under a moderate broiler (grill) for about 5 minutes until reheated and beginning to brown.

Garnish with any leftover filling ingredients and serve with salads.

Preparation time about 15 minutes

Cooking time about 1½ hours

Serves 4

Note: Halve very large potatoes before cooking to save time.

TRADITIONAL POTATO SALAD

1¹/₂–2 lb (675–900 g) new potatoes
   in their skins, scrubbed
salt and freshly ground black
   pepper
6 tablespoons thick mayonnaise
2 tablespoons French dressing (see
   page 58)
1–2 tablespoons sour cream,
   plain (natural) yogurt or
   fromage frais
1 clove garlic, crushed (optional)
4 level tablespoons snipped chives
   or ¹/₂ bunch scallions (shallots),
   trimmed and thinly sliced
mixed lettuce leaves to garnish
scallion (shallot) tassels to garnish

Cook potatoes in salted water for about 15–20 minutes until tender. Drain and allow to cool a little.

Whisk together mayonnaise, French dressing, sour cream, seasonings and garlic (if using) until well emulsified.

Cut potatoes into large cubes or, if small, leave whole or halved. Add to mayonnaise mixture while still hot and toss evenly. Add chives and mix well. Leave until cold.

Arrange lettuce leaves in a bowl or on a plate and spoon salad on top. Garnish with onion tassels.

Preparation time about 25 minutes

Cooking time 15–20 minutes

Serves 4–6

Note: The potatoes may be peeled, or cooked in their skins and then peeled if preferred.

Variations: A traditional salad can become a special treat with the addition of; a can of anchovy fillets, well-drained and chopped; 2 tablespoons of capers to the dressing; 8–12 sliced and pitted black olives and 8–12 sliced pimiento-stuffed green olives; 1 small, thinly sliced red (salad) onion and 1–2 tablespoons of freshly chopped cilantro (fresh coriander leaves) in place of the chives.

TURKISH LAMB STEW

1 tablespoon olive oil
1¹/₂ lb (675 g) lean lamb, cut into
    about ³/₄ in (2 cm) cubes
4 onions, peeled and cut into
    wedges
2 cloves garlic, crushed
1¹/₂ lb (675 g) potatoes, peeled and
    cut into large cubes
12 oz (350 g) tomatoes, peeled and
    sliced or quartered
1 red or green bell pepper
    (capsicum), seeded and sliced
3³/₄ cups (30 fl oz, 900 ml) lamb or
    beef stock or water
2 tablespoons wine vinegar
2 fresh bay leaves
1 level teaspoon freshly chopped
    sage or ¹/₂ level teaspoon
    dried sage
1 level tablespoon freshly chopped
    dill or fennel or 1 level teaspoon
    dried dillweed
salt and freshly ground black
    pepper
1 medium eggplant (aubergine),
    about 12 oz (350 g), trimmed
    and diced
12 pitted black olives

Heat oil in a large heavy-based saucepan. Add lamb and fry until well sealed.

Add onions and garlic and fry for about 5 minutes until tender. Add potato, tomato, bell pepper, stock and vinegar and bring to a boil. Add bay leaves, sage and dill and season well. Cover pan and simmer gently for 1 hour.

Give stew a good stir, add eggplant and olives and adjust seasonings. Bring back to a boil, cover and simmer gently for 45–60 minutes until very tender, giving an occasional stir. Discard bay leaves.

Serve stew with plenty of crusty bread and a mixed salad, if liked.

Preparation time about 15 minutes

Cooking time 1³/₄–2 hours

Serves 5–6

Note: A chopped bulb of Florence fennel may be added or used in place of the eggplant.

VICHYSSOISE

3 tablespoons (1¹/₂ oz, 40 g) butter
    or margarine
3 large leeks, trimmed of most
    green and finely sliced
1 onion, peeled and thinly sliced
1 lb (450 g) potatoes, peeled and
    diced
3³/₄ cups (30 fl oz, 900 ml) chicken
    or vegetable stock
salt and white pepper
¹/₄ level teaspoon ground
    coriander
1 egg yolk
²/₃ cup (5 fl oz, 150 ml) light
    (single) cream
snipped chives to garnish

Melt butter in a large saucepan and sauté leek and onions very gently for about 5 minutes without browning.

Add potato, stock, seasonings and coriander and bring to a boil. Cover and simmer gently for about 30 minutes or until vegetables are very tender.

Cool a little, then sieve or puree the soup in a blender or food processor and return to a clean saucepan.

Blend the yolk with cream and whisk evenly into soup. Reheat gently without boiling, adjust seasonings, cool and chill thoroughly.

Sprinkle liberally with snipped chives and serve.

Preparation time about 15 minutes

Cooking time about 40 minutes

Serves 6

Note: This classic dish may also be served hot. Simply serve the soup as is after reheating; or thinly slice some of the green discarded part of the leek, boil in salted water for about 5 minutes until tender, drain thoroughly and stir into the soup before serving.

PERFECT POTATOES — EACH TIME

PREPARATION

Once peeled or scrubbed, all potatoes should be cooked as soon as possible by whatever method chosen, or they will go brown. If you must keep peeled potatoes before cooking, add the juice of half a lemon to cold water and soak; and remember to rinse and add fresh water before cooking. Cut to uniform sizes and cut large potatoes into small even pieces to reduce cooking times and ensure even cooking.

BOILING

When boiling, add a pinch of salt to the water, and new potatoes are enhanced by the addition of a few sprigs of mint. Boil until just tender if serving whole, drain quickly and serve piping hot, tossed with butter and chopped parsley or herbs.

MASHING

Use a floury variety of potato and boil until very tender to prevent any lumps left in the finished potatoes.

MICROWAVING

The microwave is ideal for cooking small potatoes to serve whole, potatoes cut into wedges to serve whole, or for cooking potatoes that are to be mashed. The sizes must be uniform, the container microwave–proof. Add 3 tablespoons water and cover the bowl with plastic wrap (cling film) with a slit in it. Allow 9–10 minutes on maximum (100%).

CHIPS (FRENCH FRIES)

Allow 6–8 oz (150–225 g) potatoes per head. Peel, cut into even slices about $1/4$–$1/3$ inch (5mm–10mm) thick and cut slices into even strips. Soak in cold water for $1/2$ an hour. Drain thoroughly and dry with a clean cloth or paper towel. Heat oil in a pan suitable for deep–frying to about 385°F (196°C), place a few chips in a frying basket and lower gently into hot fat. Cook for 4–5 minutes until beginning to brown, remove from oil. Reheat oil and return chips to pan until golden. Drain on crumpled paper towel and serve very hot.

CREAMED POTATOES

Use floury potatoes, allowing 5–8 oz (150–225 g) per head. Cut into even-sized pieces and cook in boiling salted water for 10–15 minutes until tender; or microwave (as described above). Drain thoroughly and mash by hand, in a blender or food processor, with a large hand held electric mixer or press through a sieve. Season with salt and pepper, and other spices or herbs if liked. Beat in 1–2 oz (30–60 g) butter or margarine per 1 lb (450 g) potatoes and 4–5 tablespoons hot milk (the amount needed varies depending on the type of potatoes used). Beat over heat until potatoes are really fluffy. Single or double cream may be used in place of or combined with milk.

CRISPS

Slice peeled potatoes into very thin slices. Deep-fry in hot fat or oil 395°F (202°C) until golden brown. Drain on paper towel, season with salt and serve hot or leave until cold and crisp.

DUCHESSE POTATOES

Useful for piping around savory dishes as a border, or into shapes such as whirls or small baskets to fill with cooked vegetables. Boil 1 lb (450 g) potatoes until tender, drain and press through a sieve. Beat in 1 oz (30 g) softened butter and 1–2 tablespoons cream followed by 1 beaten egg and plenty of seasonings. When cool enough to handle put into a piping bag fitted with a large star vegetable nozzle and pipe shapes and sizes required onto greased baking sheets. Place in a hot oven (425°F, 220°C, Gas Mark 7) for 10–20 minutes or until lightly browned.

ROAST POTATOES

It is best to peel the potatoes first, although not essential. Allow 4–6 oz (100–175 g) potatoes per head.

Cut into even–sized pieces about the size of a small egg and dust lightly with salt. Melt about 3 oz (75 g) dripping in a roasting tin or heat about 4–6 tablespoons oil, add potatoes, turning in the hot fat. Bake in a hot oven (425°F, 220°C, Gas Mark 7) for 1–$1^1/4$ hours until tender and golden, turning them halfway through cooking so they brown evenly.

Alternately, parboil for 8 minutes in salted water; drain thoroughly. Add to hot fat as above, and cook in hot oven for about 45 minutes until golden brown. (Both raw or parboiled potatoes can be added to the juices around a roasting joint.)

WEDGES

Scrub 2–3 potatoes, about 8 oz (225 g) each, and cut in half. Cutting so all pieces are lengthwise, halve again to give quarters and in halve again to give 8 wedges. Place in a single layer in a microwave-proof dish and microwave as described above.

INDEX